For my very special Friend

With love from

Other books in this series:
Thank you Mum
I've got a crush on you
Have a Perfect Day
My Dad, My Hero
Stay Calm

Published in 2010 by Helen Exley Giftbooks in Great Britain. A copy of the CIP data is available from the British Library on request. All rights reserved. No part of this publication may be reproduced or transmitted in any form or by any means, electronic or mechanical, including photocopy, recording or any information storage and retrieval system without permission in writing from the Publisher.
Printed in China.

Words and illustrations © Jenny Kempe 2010
Design and arrangement © Exley Publications 2010
The moral right of the author has been asserted.

12 11 10 9 8 7 6 5 4 3

ISBN: 978-1-84634-488-6

Dedication: To Jullan, my best friend forever.

Published by HELEN EXLEY®
Helen Exley Giftbooks, 16 Chalk Hill, Watford, Herts WD19 4BG, UK.
www.helenexleygiftbooks.com

Best Friends

WORDS AND ILLUSTRATIONS BY
JENNY KEMPE

When I'm with my friend
I feel happy.

We share the same interests;
Have the same point of view.

My friend forgives me

for the stupid things I've said.

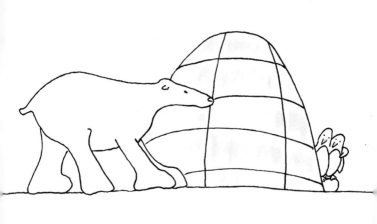

My friend protects me
when I am feeling
exposed and vulnerable.

My friend thinks I am beautiful
and deserve the best.

My friend encourages me
to follow my dreams.

My friend brings out the best in me.

We support each other.
We learn together.

Sometimes we get
ourselves into situations
we can't get out of.

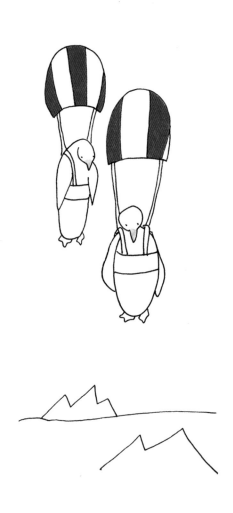

With my friend I am fearless.

With my friend I do things
I could never do on my own.

We don't always have to talk.
Sometimes we can just be.

Without my friend I'm lonely.

My friend and I
share moments
I will remember forever.

Even when the whole world
turns its back on me
my friend is still my friend.

When I'm with my friend
I feel special.

we're best

friends forever.

Jenny Kempe

In 2009, overwhelmed by the endless bad news in the media, Jenny Kempe decided to take a six month break from newspapers, TV and radio. She turned her focus to the things in life that made her happy; to friends and family and to "taking time to just be". The result is the wonderfully bright and positive gift book series "Life is Beautiful". Each title has been designed to warm your heart and to put a smile on your face. As gifts, these books will brighten up the day, or even the life, of someone you care for.

About Helen Exley gifts

Helen Exley products cover the most powerful range of all human relationships: love between couples, the bonds within families and between friends. No expense is spared in making sure that each book is as thoughtful and meaningful a gift as it is possible to create: good to give, good to receive. You have the result in your hands. If you have loved it – tell others!

Visit our website to see all of Helen Exley's other books and gifts: **www.helenexleygiftbooks.com**

Helen Exley Giftbooks
16 Chalk Hill, Watford, Herts
WD19 4BG, UK
www.helenexleygiftbooks.com

We loved making this book for you.
We hope you'll enjoy the other titles
in our series Life is Beautiful.

The Life is Beautiful Team